Code Talker

A Novel Study

By Jane Kotinek

ISBN -13: 978-1478337874   ISBN-10: 1478337877

Table of Contents

Code Talker A Novel Study
Introduction

During World War II, the United States government realized they needed a different means to send coded messages to their commanders concerning strategic maneuvers and battle plans. The government made the decision to use Navajo Marines.

The Navajo language is a very difficult language to learn if you are not a native speaker. The U.S. government enlisted Navajos so they could create a code using their language. It has been said that the U.S. would not have won the war against Japan if it had not been for the Navajo code talkers.

Code Talker, by Joseph Bruchac, is the story of Ned Begay, a Navajo code talker during World War II. Begay joined the Marines at the age of 16 (he lied about his age). While at Boot Camp, Begay is chosen to be a part of the Code Talker program. Begay describes his experiences at Boot Camp, during code talker training, and while in the battlefield. He tells his story in a humorous, poignant way that draws the reader into it. Throughout the story, Begay demonstrates how he keeps his Navajo ways close while trying to fit into the world outside his reservation.

K-W-L Chart

Directions: Complete the chart with as much information as you can.

K What I Know	W What I want to know	L What I learned
*World War II- The U.S. was fighting against Japan after they attacked Pearl Harbor. *Japan was allies with Germany and Italy. *The Navajos were Indians.		

Background Information

Directions: Read the *Author's Notes* on pages 215- 224. Answer the following questions.

1. Where do ethnologists believe the Navajos originated from?

    _____

    _____

    _____

    _____

2. What makes up the Four Corners area?

    _____

3. Why does the author believe the Navajos were not warlike raiders?

    _____

    _____

4. Why did the New Mexicans wish for the U.S. to engage in warfare against the Navajos?

    _____

5. Describe the Navajo Long Walk.

    _____

    _____

    _____

    _____

6. Where were the Navajos allowed to return after they promised to never fight against the U.S. again?

    _____

7. Why did most people not know about the important role the Navajos played in WWII?

    _____

    _____

Vocabulary List

1. chaos (104)

2. crucial (135)

3. defiant (25)

4. deployed (151)

5. distorted (153)

6. embark (89)

7. fiery (15)

8. fluently (45)

9. furloughs (69)

10. harmony (139)

11. humble (82)

12. inaccurate (147)

13. pathetic (97)

14. praised (87)

15. priority (95)

16. retreated (127)

17. reverberated (47)

18. shelling (114)

19. stealthily (124)

20. surged (117)

Vocabulary List with Definitions

chaos	great confusion or disorder
crucial	vital, extremely important
defiant	disobedient, rebellious
deployed	arranged, left, set out
distorted	warped, unclear, hazy
embark	board, get on
fiery	hot, flaming, easily excited
fluently	smoothly, effortlessly
furlough	leave of absence, vacation, unpaid leave
harmony	accord, agreement
humble	modest, unassuming
inaccurate	wrong, mistaken
pathetic	sad, dismal, useless
praised	admire, honor, congratulate
priority	main concern, most important
retreated	move back, withdraw, run away
reverberated	echo continuously
shelling	gunfire, shooting
stealthily	furtively, silently, quietly, without detection
surged	rush, pour, gush

Vocabulary Activity #1

chaos	embark	humble	retreated
crucial	fiery	inaccurate	reverberated
defiant	fluently	pathetic	shelling
deployed	furloughs	praised	stealthily
distorted	harmony	priority	surged

Directions: Unscramble the vocabulary word and write it on the space provided.

1. fnfdeia _____
2. prrtyiio _____
3. uersgd _____
4. eeeerrradtbv _____
5. mnyrhao _____
6. aieprsd _____
7. yrfei _____
8. shcao _____
9. ccrtneaai _____
10. kbrmea _____
11. ieacphtt _____
12. cclraiu _____
13. lltyfneu _____
14. eeeadrrtt _____
15. llngiehs _____
16. eeoyddlp _____
17. ylihtlaets _____
18. mbleuh _____
19. lrufshguo _____
20. stiddorte _____

Vocabulary Activity #2

chaos	embark	humble	retreated
crucial	fiery	inaccurate	reverberated
defiant	fluently	pathetic	shelling
deployed	furloughs	praised	stealthily
distorted	harmony	priority	surged

Directions: Find the missing vowels for each vocabulary word and write the vocabulary word on the space provided.

1. h__mbl__ _____

2. r__v__rb__r__t__d _____

3. fl__ __ntl__ _____

4. r__tr__ __t__d _____

5. __mb__rk _____

6. sh__ll__ng _____

7. cr__c__ __l _____

8. d__f__ __nt _____

9. d__st__rt__d _____

10. pr__ __r__ty _____

11. f__rl__ __ghs _____

12. s__rg__d _____

13. st__ __lth__l__ _____

14. d__pl__ __ __d _____

15. f__ __r__ _____

16. __n__cc__r__t__ _____

17. pr__ __s__d _____

18. h__rm__ny _____

19. p__th__t__c _____

20. ch__ __s _____

Vocabulary Activity #3

Directions: Use the dictionary guide words to decide whether the vocabulary word falls before the first guide word, between the guide words, or after the guide words. Place an X in the correct box.

Vocabulary Word	Guide Words	Before Guide Words	Between Guide Words	After Guide Words
chaos	cap/care			
crucial	crow/crust			
defiant	deny/depth			
deployed	depress/dervish			
distorted	dissent/distant			
embark	elope/embed			
fiery	field/figure			
fluently	fluid/flush			
furloughs	fun/fuse			
harmony	hard/harm			
humble	humor/hurry			
inaccurate	impulse/inaugural			
pathetic	past/paten			
praised	powder/prairie			
priority	primitive/prism			
retreated	return/review			
reverberated	retch/return			
shelling	shed/shepherd			
stealthily	status/steal			
surged	surf/sushi			

Vocabulary Crossword Puzzle

Across

1. sad, dismal, useless
3. accord, agreement
7. furtively, silently, quietly, without detection
9. vital, extremely important
11. _ board, get on
12. disobedient, rebellious
15. wrong, mistaken
16. smoothly, effortlessly
17. gunfire, shooting   14. arranged, left, set out

Down

2. modest, unassuming
4. move back, withdraw, run away
5. main concern, most important
6. to echo continuously
7. rush, pour, gush
8. warped, unclear, hazy
10. admire, honor, congratulate
13. leave of absence, vacation, unpaid leave
16. hot, flaming, easily excited
18. great confusion or disorder

<u>Code Talker</u> A Novel Study

Chapter 1

1. What is a Hogan?

   _____

2. Who is the narrator?

   _____

3. What does his name mean?

   _____

4. Where was he traveling to?

   _____

   _____

5. Why did the Americans declare war on the Navajos Indians?

   _____

   _____

   _____

6. What was the long walk?

   _____

   _____

7. Describe the conditions in which the Navajo were allowed to go back to their homeland.

   _____

   _____

   _____

Essay Question: Describe the sacrifices the Navajo had to make. How would you feel if you were forced to live by someone else's rules?

_____

_____

_____

_____

_____

_____

_____

Chapter 2

1. How did Kii Yazhi and his uncle get to the school?

    _____

2. What did the jewelry worn by the Navajos symbolize?

    _____

3. Why wasn't it easy to understand the Navajo spoken by the children at the mission?

    _____

    _____

4. How are the Navajo children taught to react to adults?

    _____

5. Describe the white man who met the Navajo children.

    _____

    _____

    _____

6. Why did the white man think the children were being disrespectful to him when he was yelling at them?

    _____

7. What did Jacob Benally tell the children that shocked them?

    _____

    _____

    _____

8. Who was the white man who spoke to the children upon their arrival?

    _____

    _____

9. What did he tell the children?

    _____

    _____

Essay Question: How would you feel if you were forced to learn a different language, culture, and life because others thought your culture wasn't as good as theirs?

_____

_____

_____

_____

_____

_____

_____

_____

_____

_____

Chapter 3

1. Why did the Navajo consider their long hair to be sacred?

   _____

   _____

2. What were the children forced to wear?

   _____

3. Why do you think the school made the children get their hair cut and different clothes to wear?

   _____

   _____

   _____

4. What job did Mr. Reamer have?

   _____

5. Why was being given a new name so traumatic for the kids?

   _____

   _____

6. What name was given to the narrator?

   _____

Essay Question: How would you react if someone decided to call you by another name and you had no choice but to respond to it? Would it make you feel isolated from your family?

_____

_____

_____

_____

_____

_____

_____

_____

_____

_____

_____

Chapter 4

1. What happened to Ned when he greeted Mr. Reamer with a Navajo greeting?

   _____

   _____

2. What happened to the children who refused to stop talking Navajo?

   _____

3. Explain what happened to John Roanhorse.

   _____

   _____

   _____

4. How did Ned defy the teachers at the mission?

   _____

   _____

5. Why did Ned refuse to give up his language?

   _____

   _____

Chapter 5

1. Who was Jim Thorpe?

   _____

2. Why did Ned resent the way the teachers treated him?

   _____

   _____

3. How did having a goal make the time go faster for Ned?

   _____

   _____

4. Where was the Navajo High School located?

   _____

5. What did Ned like about the Navajo High School besides its location?

   _____

   _____

6. What is *ironic* about Ned and his classmates collecting food for the poor people of Japan?

   _____

   _____

Essay Question: Ned believes that education was a way for him to succeed and help his people. Do you believe education can lead to success? If so, why do you think so many students do not try to succeed more at education?

_____

_____

_____

_____

_____

_____

_____

_____

_____

_____

_____

_____

Chapter 6

1. What did the Japanese believe was their destiny?

   _____

   _____

2. Who did Japan form an alliance with?

   _____

3. What did the piece of paper in Ned's wallet say the Navajo Indians would do if needed?

   _____

   _____

4. What was the date of the attack on Pearl Harbor?

   _____

5. What is a dunce cap?

   _____

Chapter 7

1. Why couldn't most of the Navajo Indians fight in the war against Japan?

   _____

2. Who were the Axis powers?

   _____

3. What type of Indians were the federal Bureau of Indian Affairs looking for?

   _____

4. What impressed the boys as they looked at the Marine poster?

   _____

   _____

5. What did Ned decided about First Sergeant Shinn after observing him speak?

   _____

   _____

6. How did Ned plan to get around the age requirement?

   _____

7. What did his parents tell him?

   _____

Essay Question: What does it say about Ned that he would lie about his age to become a soldier? Do you think you would be as loyal to a country that tried to take away your land and your language? How do you think Ned's opinion of the white man will change once he joins the Marines?

_____

_____

_____

_____

_____

_____

_____

_____

_____

_____

_____

_____

_____

_____

Chapter 8

1. How many Navajos were chosen for the first group?

   _____

2. Why were the men's families getting worried about them?

   _____

3. When did the families stop worrying about the men in the 382nd?

   _____

   _____

4. What did assignment did Johnny have to do?

   _____

5. Why didn't it surprise Ned that none of the Navajos had washed out of boot camp?

   _____

   _____

Chapter 9

1. Why did Ned's parent insist he have The Blessingway ceremony done before he left?

   _____

   _____

2. Who would perform the ceremony?

   _____

3. Why did Ned like him?

   _____

   _____

4. Why did Ned feel grateful for the Blessingway ceremony?

   _____

   _____

5. How did Ned feel in the morning at the end of the ceremony?

   _____

   _____

   _____

Chapter 10

1. How did Ned justify being old enough to join the Marines?

   _____

   _____

2. Why would the Indians have felt strange at Fort Defiance?

   _____

   _____

3. Describe what happened on the first real day of boot camp.

   _____

   _____

   _____

4. Why did the Navajo look at the razors with a bit of confusion?

   _____

5. Why was Ned offended by the way the drill instructor spoke to the recruits?

   _____

6. Why did Ned find boot camp relatively easy?

_____

_____

7. What did Ned not like in boot camp training?

_____

_____

8. What did Ned fear the most in boot camp?

_____

9. How were the Navajos taught to swim?

_____

_____

10. How did Ned get across the swimming pool?

_____

11. What were some of the things Ned learned about white men during boot camp?

_____

_____

_____

_____

_____

Essay Question: How do you like the way the story is being told? Do you feel as though the narrator is speaking directly to you, the reader? Do you feel as though you are being drawn into the story? Explain your answers.

_____

_____

_____

_____

_____

_____

_____

_____

_____

Chapter 11

1. Why were Marines nicknames *leathernecks*?

_____

2. Why did Ned think the Navajo Indians were tougher than non-Indian Marines?

_____

_____

3. Where were the Navajos taken?

_____

_____

_____

4. What were they going to learn to become in the classroom?

_____

5. What was the responsibility of the code talker?

_____

_____

_____

6. Why did the Americans need to create a new code?

_____

_____

7. Who was responsible for bringing the Navajo language to the attention of the Marines?

_____

Chapter 12

1. Where were the codes stored?

_____

2. How did the Navajo code work?

_____

_____

_____

_____

_____

3. Why did Ned consider the time spent at Camp Elliott some of the best times of his life?

_____

_____

_____

4. Why did Ned keep the pollen pouch with him throughout the war?

_____

5. How would you describe the relationship the Navajos had with the non-Indians at Camp Elliot?

_____

_____

Chapter 13

1. Who would Ned be training with in Hawaii?

_____

2. Why were the Navajos never given promotions in the Marines?

_____

_____

3. Why would Mr. Lawson have made such a comment about Ned concerning his never going anywhere?

_____

4. Why didn't the Navajos eat fish?

_____

5. How did the Navajos use their teams to send, translate, and receive code?

_____

_____

_____

6. How did the Navajos update the code when needed?

_____

_____

7. What happened when the code talkers sent a test message the first time?

_____

_____

_____

8. How long did it take to send the first message?

_____

9. How long did it take to send a message using the white code?

_____

Essay Question: Considering how important their assignment was and how much it helped during the war, do you think it was fair the code talkers were never promoted?

_____
_____
_____
_____
_____
_____
_____
_____
_____
_____
_____

Chapter 14

1. Why did the Navajos try to avoid the corpses?

_____
_____

2. How were the Navajos able to deal with the dead bodies?

_____
_____

3. What were the five rules of combat every Japanese soldier was expected to follow?

_____
_____
_____
_____
_____
_____

Internal/External Conflicts

Directions: Ned experiences many conflicts occurring within the story. Complete the chart below to demonstrate your understanding of the conflicts taking place in the novel. Put your choice of a conflict occurring in the story in the last box.

Conflict	Explanation of Conflict
Ned vs. himself	
Navajos traditions vs. Marine traditions	
Ned vs. Marines	
America vs. Japan	
_____ vs. _____	

Chapter 15

1. How did the Navajos walk the desert without drinking their water?

   _____

   _____

2. Why didn't the Navajos tell the other Marines where they had gotten water?

   _____

   _____

3. What is the unwritten rule concerning war?

   _____

4. Where did the Marines practice beach landing?

   _____

5. List some of the dangerous creatures that could be found on the island.

   _____

   _____

6. Why did Ned think his conversation with Gene-gene was one of the best he had ever had even
   though they never really spoke?

   _____

   _____

   _____

Chapter 16

1. What was the name given to the Bougainville invasion?

   _____

2. Why would it be important for the Allies to have a successful invasion of Bougainville?

   _____

   _____

   _____

3. Give the actual meaning for the following code names:

   A. Alligator: _____

   B. Men's names: _____

   C. Women's names: _____

   D. Zekes: _____

E. Val: _____

F. Kate: _____

G. Betty: _____

4. Why were nicknames used for planes, bombers, and submarines?

_____

_____

5. What obstacle did the Americans face when landing on Empress Augusta Bay on Bougainville?

_____

_____

6. Describe the *battle of the Four Sitting Ducks*?

_____

_____

_____

_____

_____

_____

_____

7. How did the Marines deal with their nervousness on the morning before the D-day attack?

_____

_____

_____

_____

_____

8. How does the author build suspense while describing the pre-battle scene of D-day?

_____

_____

_____

Chapter 17

1. How many Marines were in the initial landing?

   _____

2. Why did Ned carry his radio on his chest?

   _____

3. What prompted the Marines to do what needed to be done once they landed on the beach?

   _____

   _____

4. Who had been with Ned when they landed on the beach?

   _____

5. Why hadn't the Japanese been killed in the pre-battle strikes by the planes?

   _____

   _____

6. At the end of the day, what was the thought that struck Ned concerning the battle?

   _____

   _____

Chapter 18

1. Describe the conditions of the area where the Marines were camped?

   _____

   _____

   _____

   _____

2. What is malaria?

   _____

3. How did Officer Williams ensure the Navajos were taking their Atabrine?

   _____

   _____

   _____

4. What is a banzai attack?

_____

_____

_____

5. Why was night the most dangerous time for the Marines?

_____

_____

6. What could happen if you left your foxhole during the night?

_____

_____

7. How had Harry Tsosie been killed?

_____

_____

8. How old was Ned on November 10?

_____

9. Could you imagine fighting in the Marines at 17? How would you handle seeing people you knew and didn't know being killed?

_____

_____

_____

_____

10. Explain what C-rations were.

_____

_____

11. What did the Japanese start doing with the things they left behind?

_____

_____

12. What were four rules of sending messages while in the field?

_____

13. Why were the four rules important to follow?

_____

_____

14. What was the responsibility of the Seabees?

_____

_____

15. Which Kennedy did Smitty want to introduce Ned to?

_____

Essay Question: Imagine yourself, at seventeen, fighting in a war. Do you think you could handle the horrors you would see, the discipline needed, and the courage to defend your country? Describe the personal traits possessed by you that would help you if you were in the same situation.

_____

_____

_____

_____

_____

_____

_____

_____

_____

_____

_____

_____

_____

_____

_____

_____

_____

_____

Chapter 19

1. What problem was the military facing in regards to the code talkers?

   _____

   _____

2. Describe the incident that changed the captain's mind about code talkers.

   _____

   _____

   _____

   _____

3. What was a danger for a code talker if he had to deliver a message on foot?

   _____

   _____

4. "Never think that war is a good thing, grandchildren. Though I may be necessary at times to defend our people, war is a sickness that must be cured." Page 139.

   _____

   _____

   _____

   _____

   _____

5. What did a lot of Marines, code talkers included, do to forget the horrors they had witnessed on the battlefield?

   _____

Chapter 20

1. What did the Marines who had lost their equipment at Saipan do once the fighting grew calm?

   _____

   _____

2. What did the Japanese civilians do when they saw the Americans?

   _____

   _____

3. Why did they act this way?

_____

_____

4. How many Americans died between June 15 and July 13 on Saipan? How many Japanese?

_____

5. How does the author release tension in his story?

_____

_____

Chapter 21

1. What scared Ned on Kwajalein and Eniwetok?

_____

2. What did Admiral Conolly do differently at Guam that helped the Marines?

_____

_____

3. Who were the Chamorros?

_____

_____

4. What happened to the Chamorros if they didn't help the Japanese?

_____

_____

5. "Never forget, grandchildren, that we must always see all other people as human beings, worthy of respect." What does this quote mean and why is it relevant for a book on war?

_____

_____

_____

6. How would you describe the relationship between Smitty and Ned?

_____

_____

7. How many Japanese were on Guam?

_____

8. When did the Japanese prefer to strike the enemy?

_____

9. How did Ned compare what happened to the Chamorros to what had happened to the Navajos?

_____

_____

_____

10. Who did the code talkers take care of?

_____

11. Describe what happened to Charlie Begay.

_____

_____

_____

_____

Essay Question: How do you think Ned deals with the suffering of others given his tribes history of mistreatment by whites? Does it surprise you he did not endure more prejudice while in the Marines? What does this say about the men he fought alongside?

_____

_____

_____

_____

_____

_____

_____

_____

_____

_____

_____

_____

_____

Cause and Effect Activity

Directions: Complete the cause and effect relationships listed below.

Cause	Effect
Ned was forced to attend school off the reservation.	
	Ned was given a new name.
	Ned was able to join the Marines.

Essay Question: Explain how the cause/effect relationships move the story along.

_____

_____

_____

_____

_____

_____

_____

_____

Chapter 22

1. How were the Marines like the vehicles they received to use?

_____

_____

_____

2. How did Ned get injured?

_____

_____

3. Who ran Ned to the medic?

_____

4. What is "battle fatigue?"

_____

_____

_____

5. Where did Ned go after he left the hospital?

_____

Chapter 23

1. What is DDT?

_____

_____

2. What other creature was on the island other than the land crabs?

_____

3. What are frogmen?

_____

4. Explain what kamikazes were.

_____

_____

5. Why weren't pictures of dead American soldiers shown to civilians until 1943?

_____

_____

6. How did the idea of kamikazes come about?

_____

_____

_____

_____

7. What does Kamikaze mean when translated?

_____

8. Why did Japanese men volunteer to be kamikaze pilots?

_____

_____

_____

9. Explain what the Geneva Convention rules were during war.

_____

_____

_____

10. How did the rules from Geneva go against what the Japanese believed?

_____

_____

_____

11. Why did the Americans try blockades against Japan?

_____

_____

12. Where Navajos used in other jobs besides as a code talker? If so, what did they do?

_____

_____

13. What was usually the nickname for any Indian?

_____

Chapter 24

1. Why did the Americans decide they needed Iwo Jima?

   _____

   _____

2. Describe Iwo Jima.

   _____

   _____

   _____

3. How did the Japanese fight differently on Iwo Jima?

   _____

   _____

4. What was a sennimbari?

   _____

   _____

Chapter 25

1. Why didn't the bombs dropped on Iwo Jima affect the Japanese soldiers?

   _____

   _____

2. What did the Marines find in the tunnels that angered them?

   _____

   _____

3. How many ships sailed to Iwo Jima?

   _____

4. Why did the cooks tell the Marines to enjoy their last meal before the soldiers were to start an attack?

   _____

   _____

5. Why didn't Ned eat before the attack on Iwo Jima?

   _____

   _____

6. What response did the Americans receive after they started to bomb Iwo Jima right before the soldiers landed?

_____

7. How had Iwo Jima been made?

_____

8. Why did Ned think their arrival onto the island had been too easy?

_____

_____

Essay Question: How do you think Ned felt when he saw the canned goods in the Japanese tunnels? Consider the circumstances when he and the other Navajos collected the food for the Japanese.

_____

_____

_____

_____

_____

_____

_____

_____

_____

_____

Chapter 26

1. What happened once the troops had arrived on the beach and climbed the first slope?

_____

_____

2. Describe the smells Ned remembers from Iwo Jima.

_____

_____

_____

_____

3. What was the major objective on the island?

_____

4. Why was the raising of the American flag so significant to the Marines who saw it flying?

_____

_____

5. How many Marines were injured at Iwo Jima?

_____

6. What does Ned mean when he says, "I say "too many" because having a lot of friends during war can be a painful thing?"

_____

_____

_____

7. What happened to Georgia Boy?

_____

_____

8. Why didn't medics where the red cross symbol?

_____

_____

_____

9. What did you learn about the famous picture taken at Iwo Jima?

_____

_____

_____

10. Why didn't Ira like looking at the picture of the flag being raised at Iwo Jima?

_____

_____

_____

Chapter 27

1. Why was Iwo Jima considered the key to the war ending?

   _____

   _____

2. Where was Ned sent after Iwo Jima?

   _____

3. Who was Ned happy to see on the ship?

   _____

4. Why did the landing on Okinawa beaches make the Marines nervous?

   _____

   _____

   _____

5. What was the plan of the Japanese on Okinawa?

   _____

   _____

6. How many men did the Japanese lose on Okinawa?

   _____

7. What was the Thought Police?

   _____

   _____

8. What was contained in the package sent to the Emperor by the dead soldier's family?

   _____

   _____

9. What did this act of the parents symbolize?

   _____

   _____

10. Who was the real power in Japan during the war?

    _____

11. Who was the president during the war?

    _____

Chapter 28

1. What events caused Emperor Hirohito to go to the Supreme Council and agree to surrender?

   _____

2. What was the date that Japan surrendered to America?

   _____

3. What did the code talkers do after hearing about the surrender?

   _____

Chapter 29

1. What had the bombs done to the buildings and people of Japan?

   _____

   _____

2. What was the designated code for the code talkers?

   _____

3. How was Ned treated, while wearing his uniform, when he entered the bar?

   _____

   _____

4. What did Ned realize after his incident at the bar?

   _____

   _____

5. What had Ned learned in the Marines?

   _____

   _____

6. What did Ned mean when he said he needed to heal after the war?

   _____

   _____

   _____

7. What occupation did Ned do after the war?

   _____

8. Why couldn't the Indians use the G.I. Bill to build a new home?

   _____

   _____

9. When were the code talkers allowed to discuss their contribution to the war?

_____

Essay Question: How do you feel about the fact that the Navajos were good enough to lose their lives fighting for the United States, but they were still discriminated against after the war? Explain your answer.

_____

_____

_____

_____

_____

_____

_____

_____

_____

_____

_____

_____

_____

_____

Compare/Contrast Activity

Directions: Compare and contrast (show the similarities and differences) between the treatment of the Navajos in the United States and their treatment while in the Marines. Use at least 3 examples for each.

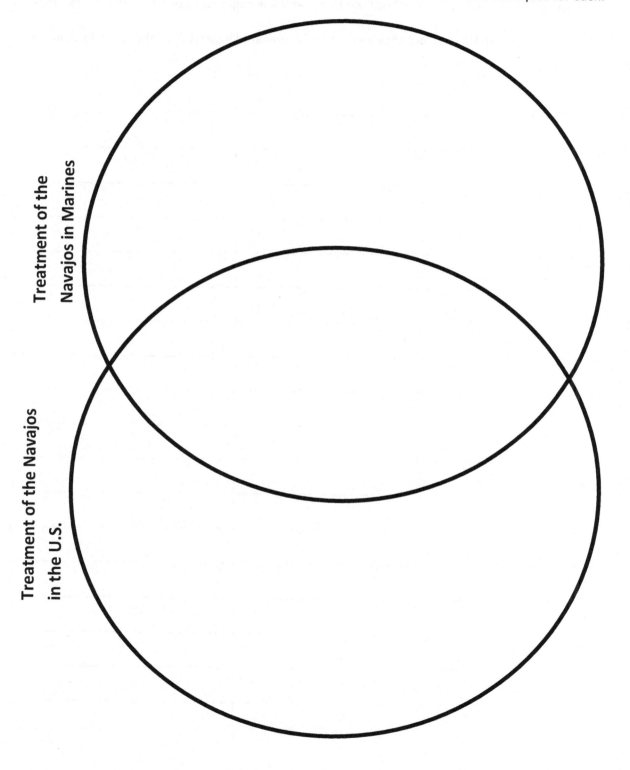

Treatment of the Navajos in Marines

Treatment of the Navajos in the U.S.

Compare/Contrast Activity

Directions: Using the Venn Diagram above, write an essay comparing and contrasting the treatment of the Navajos in the U.S. and while in the Marines. Be sure you do not create a list in your essay. Use signal words for compare/contrast (First, for instance, compared to, etc.) to write your essay.

_____
_____
_____
_____
_____
_____
_____
_____
_____
_____
_____
_____
_____
_____
_____
_____
_____
_____
_____
_____
_____
_____
_____
_____

Plot Diagram

Directions: Starting at the beginning of the story, place the most important events in order on the plot diagram below.

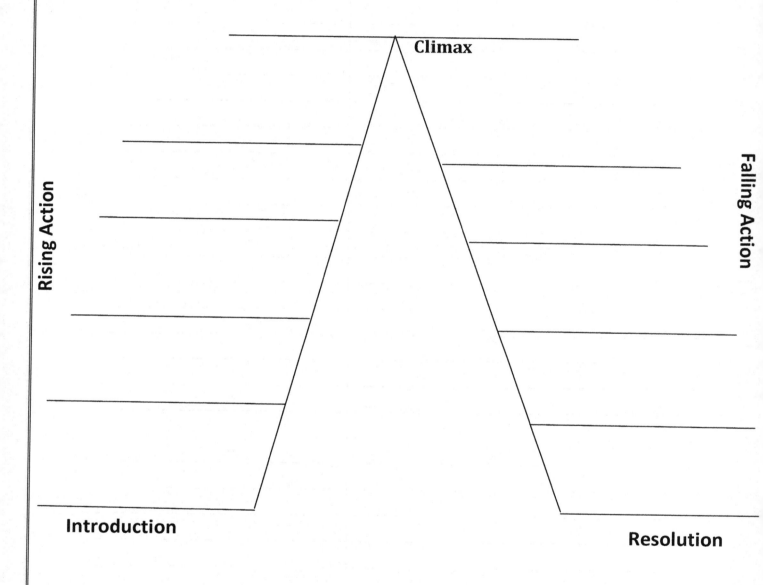

Climax

Rising Action

Falling Action

Introduction

Resolution

Analyzing Theme Activity

Directions: Discuss the theme or themes of the story.

Theme: A general idea or message normally concerned with life, human nature, or society the author is trying to relay to the reader. A theme is usually a universal idea (love vs. hate, loyalty vs. disloyalty, fairness) that is not stated directly by the author rather it is understood by the reader through the evidence provided in the storyline.

1. Brainstorm as many themes as you can for the story. Write them below.

   _____

   _____

   _____

   _____

2. Which theme idea do you feel is the most important to the story? Explain your answer.

   _____

   _____

   _____

   _____

3. Can there be more than one theme to a novel?

   _____

   _____

   _____

   _____

4. Of the themes you mention above, which one do you relate to the most and why?

   _____

   _____

Point of View Activity

Directions: Determine which point of view is being used in the novel and how it affects the telling of the story.

First-person point of view: when the narrator uses the pronouns "I" when telling the story.

Limited third-person point of view: the narrator tells the story from the perspective of one or more of the character(s) using the pronouns *he, she, us, we, etc.*

1. The story is written in_____ point of view.

2. In your opinion, would the use of different points of view enhance the storyline?

    _____

    _____

    _____

    _____

3. How would the story change if it were written entirely in third-person point of view?

    _____

    _____

    _____

    _____

4. Why is a story written in first-person point of view better for understanding the motive behind a character's actions?

    _____

    _____

    _____

    _____

Character Analysis Activity

Directions: The novel has provided extensive proof of Ned's personality and traits. Do you feel he showed exceptional traits throughout the story? Are there any traits he possessed that you would like to acquire? If so, explain why. What did you not like about him?

_____

_____

_____

_____

_____

_____

_____

_____

_____

_____

_____

_____

_____

_____

_____

_____

_____

_____

_____

_____

_____

_____

Teacher's Edition

Background Information- Answers

Directions: Read the *Author's Notes* on pages 215- 224. Answer the following questions.

1. Where do ethnologists believe the Navajos originated from? **The evidence points to the Navajos coming into the Southwest 1,000 years or more ago. Their language links them to the Athabaskan people of Alaska. The Navajos believe they emerged into this world from a hole in the earth. They believe the earth is only one of many they have lived in.**

2. What makes up the Four Corners area? **New Mexico, Arizona, Colorado, and Utah.**

3. Why does the author believe the Navajos were not warlike raiders? **Peace and balance were extremely important to the Navajos.**

4. Why did the New Mexicans wish for the U.S. to engage in warfare against the Navajos? **The New Mexicans wanted to continue using the Navajos as slaves.**

5. Describe the Navajo Long Walk. **It was a forced march of most of the Navajo nation to an Army post almost 400 miles across mountains and deserts. Many Navajos died during the march.**

6. Where were the Navajos allowed to return after they promised to never fight against the U.S. again? **They were allowed to return to the Four Corners.**

7. Why did most people not know about the important role the Navajos played in WWII? **It was considered top secret.**

Vocabulary Activity #1- Answers

chaos	embark	humble	retreated
crucial	fiery	inaccurate	reverberated
defiant	fluently	pathetic	shelling
deployed	furloughs	praised	stealthily
distorted	harmony	priority	surged

Directions: Unscramble the vocabulary word and write it on the space provided.

1. fnfdeia   <u>defiant</u>
2. prrtyiio   <u>priority</u>
3. uersgd   <u>surged</u>
4. eeeerrradtbv   <u>reverberated</u>
5. mnyrhao   <u>harming</u>
6. aieprsd   <u>praised</u>
7. yrfei   <u>fiery</u>
8. shcao   <u>chaos</u>
9. ccrtneaai   <u>inaccurate</u>
10. kbrmea   <u>embark</u>
11. ieacphtt   <u>embark</u>
12. cclraiu   <u>pathetic</u>
13. lltyfneu   <u>fluently</u>
14. eeeadrrtt   <u>retreated</u>
15. llngiehs   <u>shelling</u>
16. eeoyddlp   <u>deployed</u>
17. ylihtlaets   <u>stealthily</u>
18. mbleuh   <u>humble</u>
19. lrufshguo   <u>furloughs</u>
20. stiddorte   <u>distorted</u>

Vocabulary Activity #2- Answers

chaos	embark	humble	retreated
crucial	fiery	inaccurate	reverberated
defiant	fluently	pathetic	shelling
deployed	furloughs	praised	stealthily
distorted	harmony	priority	surged

Directions: Find the missing vowels for each vocabulary word and write the vocabulary word on the space provided.

1. h__mbl__   humble
2. r__v__rb__r__t__d   reverberated
3. fl__ __ntl__   fluently
4. r__tr__ __t__d   retreated
5. __mb__rk   embark
6. sh__ll__ng   shelling
7. cr__c__ __l   crucial
8. d__f__ __nt   defiant
9. d__st__rt__d   distorted
10. pr__ __r__ty   priority
11. f__rl__ __ghs   furloughs
12. s__rg__d   surged
13. st__ __lth__l__   stealthily
14. d__pl__ __ __d   deployed
15. f__ __r__   fiery
16. __n__cc__r__t__   inaccurate
17. pr__ __s__d   praised
18. h__rm__ny   harmony
19. p__th__t__c   pathetic
20. ch__ __s   chaos

Vocabulary Activity #3- Answers

Directions: Use the dictionary guide words to decide whether the vocabulary word falls before the first guide word, between the guide words, or after the guide words. Place an X in the correct box.

Vocabulary Word	Guide Words	Before Guide Words	Between Guide Words	After Guide Words
chaos	cap/care			X
crucial	crow/crust		X	
defiant	deny/depth	X		
deployed	depress/dervish	X		
distorted	dissent/distant			X
embark	elope/embed		X	
fiery	field/figure		X	
fluently	fluid/flush	X		
furloughs	fun/fuse		X	
harmony	hard/harm			X
humble	humor/hurry	X		
inaccurate	impulse/inaugural		X	
pathetic	past/paten			X
praised	powder/prairie			X
priority	primitive/prism		X	
retreated	return/review	X		
reverberated	retch/return	X		
shelling	shed/shepherd		X	
stealthily	status/steal			X
surged	surf/sushi		X	

Vocabulary Crossword Puzzle- Answers

Across

1. sad, dismal, useless
3. accord, agreement
7. furtively, silently, quietly, without detection
9. vital, extremely important
11. board, get on
12. disobedient, rebellious
15. wrong, mistaken
16. smoothly, effortlessly
17. gunfire, shooting

Down

2. modest, unassuming
4. move back, withdraw, run away
5. main concern, most important
6. to echo continuously
7. rush, pour, gush
8. warped, unclear, hazy
10. admire, honor, congratulate
13. leave of absence, vacation, unpaid leave
14. arranged, left, set out
16. hot, flaming, easily excited
18. great confusion or disorder

<u>Code Talker</u> A Novel Study

Code Talker A Novel Study

Chapter 1

1. What is a Hogan? **A home built by the Navajo.**
2. Who is the narrator? **Kii Yazhi.**
3. What does his name mean? **Little Boy.**
4. Where was he traveling to? **He was traveling to Gallup, to the mission school located there.**
5. Why did the Americans declare war on the Navajos Indians? **They would not stop raiding the Mexicans who continued to raid their villages and turn their people into slaves.**
6. What was the long walk? **The Navajo were forced to walk hundreds of miles to Fort Sumner.**
7. Describe the conditions in which the Navajo were allowed to go back to their homeland. **They had to promise to obey the American laws, stop raiding, and to learn the white-man ways.**

Essay Question: Describe the sacrifices the Navajo had to make. How would you feel if you were forced to live by someone else's rules?

Chapter 2

1. How did Kii Yazhi and his uncle get to the school? **They rode in a wagon.**
2. What did the jewelry symbolize? **It symbolized how much their families loved them.**
3. Why wasn't it easy to understand the Navajo spoken by the children at the mission? **They spoke the same language but they were from different areas and the language was slightly different.**
4. How are the Navajo children taught to react to adults? **They were taught to respect them.**
5. Describe the white man who met the Navajo children.
6. Why did the white man think the children were being disrespectful to him when he was yelling at them? **They were looking down at the ground.**
7. What did Jacob Benally tell the children that shocked them? **He told them they were no longer allowed to speak Navajo. There were to speak English or say nothing at all.**
8. Who was the white man who spoke to the children upon their arrival? **He was the principal of the mission school, Principal O'Sullivan.**
9. What did he tell the children? **Everything they knew about being Indian had to be forgotten.**

Essay Question: How would you feel if you were forced to learn a different language, culture, and life because others thought your culture wasn't as good as theirs?

Chapter 3

1. Why did the Navajo consider their long hair to be sacred? **Long hair ensured that misfortune would stay away.**
2. What were the children forced to wear? **They had to wear an uncomfortable uniform.**
3. Why do you think the school made the children get their hair cut and different clothes to wear? **Answers will vary.**
4. What job did Mr. Reamer have? **He gave the children their new American name.**
5. Why was being given a new name so traumatic for the kids? **Answers will vary.**
6. What name was given to the narrator? **Ned Begay.**

Essay Question: How would you react if someone decided to call you by another name and you had no choice but to respond to it? Would it make you feel isolated from your family?

Chapter 4

1. What happened to Ned when he greeted Mr. Reamer with a Navajo greeting? **He had his mouth washed out with soap.**
2. What happened to the children who refused to stop talking Navajo? **They were beaten with heavy sticks.**
3. Explain what happened to John Roanhorse. **He was taken to a cellar and chained in it for a week. He was given stale bread and water.**
4. How did Ned defy the teachers at the mission? **He spoke Navajo whenever he wasn't around the white folks.**
5. Why did Ned refuse to give up his language? **Answers will vary.**

Chapter 5

1. Who was Jim Thorpe? **He was a famous Indian athlete.**
2. Why did Ned resent the way the teachers treated him? **They didn't expect him to be as smart as the white children.**
3. How did having a goal make the time go faster for Ned? **He had something to achieve, to work for.**
4. Where was the Navajo High School located? **20 miles away from his home.**
5. What did Ned like about the Navajo High School besides its location? **The teachers taught them a lot more.**
6. What is *ironic* about Ned and his classmates collecting food for the poor people of Japan? **They were poor and struggled to get food for themselves.**

Essay Question: Ned believes that education was a way for him to succeed and help his people. Do you believe education can lead to success? If so, why do you think so many students do not try to succeed more at education?

Chapter 6

1. What did the Japanese believe was their destiny? **To own all the land around them.**
2. Who did Japan form an alliance with? **Germany.**
3. What did the piece of paper in Ned's wallet say the Navajo Indians would do if needed? **They would fight as Americans against anyone who threatened them.**
4. What was the date of the attack on Pearl Harbor? **December 7, 1941.**
5. What is a dunce cap? **It was a pointed hat placed on the top of a student's head.**

Chapter 7

1. Why couldn't most of the Navajo Indians fight in the war against Japan? **They didn't speak enough English.**
2. Who were the Axis powers? **Japan, Germany, and Italy.**

3. What type of Indians were the federal Bureau of Indian Affairs looking for? **Those who were fluent in both Navajo and English.**

4. What impressed the boys as they looked at the Marine poster? **They were impressed by the uniform worn by the Marine.**

5. What did Ned decided about First Sergeant Shinn after observing him speak? **He trusted him because he felt Shinn believed what he was saying.**

6. How did Ned plan to get around the age requirement? **He would lie about his age.**

7. What did his parents tell him? **He had to wait one year before they would let him join.**

Essay Question: What does it say about Ned that he would lie about his age to become a soldier? Do you think you would be as loyal to a country that tried to take away your land and your language? How do you think Ned's opinion of the white man will change once he joins the Marines?

Chapter 8

1. How many Navajos were chosen for the first group? **29 men.**

2. Why were the men's families getting worried about them? **They didn't receive any letters from the men.**

3. When did the families stop worrying about the men in the 382nd? **They stopped worrying when Corporal Johnny Manuelito showed up.**

4. What did assignment did Johnny have to do? **He was the new recruiter.**

5. Why didn't it surprise Ned that none of the Navajos had washed out of boot camp? **Navajos did on a daily basis what was expected of the men during boot camp.**

Chapter 9

1. Why did Ned's parent insist he have The Blessingway ceremony done before he left? **It would keep him safe.**

2. Who would perform the ceremony? **Hosteen Mitchell.**

3. Why did Ned like him? **He was funny and wise.**

4. Why did Ned feel grateful for the Blessingway ceremony? **He felt surrounded by love from his family and friends.**

5. How did Ned feel in the morning at the end of the ceremony? **He felt he had a good balance between his mind, body, spirit and emotions.**

Chapter 10

1. How did Ned justify being old enough to join the Marines? **He felt being 16 was old enough to fight.**

2. Why would the Indians have felt strange at Fort Defiance? **It was where the Navajo had started the Long Walk in 1863.**

3. Describe what happened on the first real day of boot camp. **They had their heads shaved. They were issued their boot camp uniforms and hygiene kit.**

4. Why did the Navajo look at the razors with a bit of confusion? **Navajo Indians did not have facial hair.**

5. Why was Ned offended by the way the drill instructor spoke to the recruits? **He swore a lot.**

6. Why did Ned find boot camp relatively easy? **He was used to the exercise. He also became aware it was simply a daily routine.**

7. What did Ned not like in boot camp training? **He didn't like boxing because it felt unnatural to hit another person.**

8. What did Ned fear the most in boot camp? **The swimming test.**

9. How were the Navajos taught to swim? **They were pushed into the deep end of the pool while blindfolded. Sink or swim.**

10. How did Ned get across the swimming pool? **He walked on the bottom.**

11. What were some of the things Ned learned about white men during boot camp? **White men are not born knowing everything. Where it matters, white men are no different than Navajos. People can always learn from one another.**

Essay Question: How do you like the way the story is being told? Do you feel as though the narrator is speaking directly to you, the reader? Do you feel as though you are being drawn into the story? Explain your answers.

Chapter 11

1. Why were Marines nicknames *leathernecks*? **They were the toughest of all the armed forces.**

2. Why did Ned think the Navajo Indians were tougher than non-Indian Marines? **They were protecting their ancestors land and their people.**

3. Where were the Navajos taken? **They were taken to Camp Elliott where they were taken to a barrack with barred windows and a locked door.**

4. What were they going to learn to become in the classroom? **Code Talkers.**

5. What was the responsibility of the code talker? **He would use the Navajo language to create a new code to be used in the war. They would send messages to other code talkers who would then translate the code for the commanders.**

6. Why did the Americans need to create a new code? **The Japanese broke all of the other codes.**

7. Who was responsible for bringing the Navajo language to the attention of the Marines? **Philip Johnson.**

Chapter 12

1. Where were the codes stored? **In the Navajos head.**

2. How did the Navajo code work? **Each letter of the English alphabet was assigned a Navajo word that, when translated, started with the English letter.**

3. Why did Ned consider the time spent at Camp Elliott some of the best times of his life? **He felt good because he was able to enjoy being a Navajo where he could speak his own language without being yelled at or punished. He felt proud that he would be able to do something for his country.**

4. Why did Ned keep the pollen pouch with him throughout the war? **It kept him balanced and calm.**

5. How would you describe the relationship the Navajos had with the non-Indians at Camp Elliot? **There were comrades. They were soldiers together. They had made good friends.**

Chapter 13

1. Who would Ned be training with in Hawaii? **The code talkers who had seen battle.**
2. Why were the Navajos never given promotions in the Marines? **The secret of the code talkers had to be kept. Also, it was still a white man's world.**
3. Why would Mr. Lawson have made such a comment about Ned concerning his never going anywhere? **Indians were not expected to succeed.**
4. Why didn't the Navajos eat fish? **Anything associated with water was considered dangerous.**
5. How did the Navajos use their teams to send, translate, and receive code? **One person would talk and another would write what was spoken. Then the code would be translated.**
6. How did the Navajos update the code when needed? **Navajos would meet at a location to update the other code talkers.**
7. What happened when the code talkers sent a test message the first time? **People thought the Japanese were attacking because they had never heard the Navajo language before.**
8. How long did it take to send the first message? **Two minutes.**
9. How long did it take to send a message using the white code? **4 hours.**

Essay Question: Considering how important their assignment was and how much it helped during the war, do you think it was fair the code talkers were never promoted?

Chapter 14

1. Why did the Navajos try to avoid the corpses? **A bad spirit had a tendency to stick around a dead body.**
2. How were the Navajos able to deal with the dead bodies? **They knew it was their duty to be able to cope with dealing with a corpse.**
3. What were the five rules of combat every Japanese soldier was expected to follow? **1. Obey without question or hesitation. 2. Always take the offensive. 3. Surprise the enemy whenever possible. 4. Never retreat. 5. Never surrender.**

Chapter 15

1. How did the Navajos walk the desert without drinking their water? **They drank the water in the cactus.**
2. Why didn't they tell the other Marines where they had gotten water? **They wanted the other Marines to think they were very tough.**
3. What is the unwritten rule concerning war? **Expect the unexpected.**
4. Where did the Marines practice beach landing? **Guadalcanal.**
5. List some of the dangerous creatures that could be found on the island. **Crocodiles, leeches, spiders, scorpions, and poisonous centipedes.**
6. Why did Ned think his conversation with Gene-gene was one of the best he had ever had even though they never really spoke? **They communicated through their love of their home.**
7. What did Ned think was wrong with the practice run onto the island? **There was no chaos.**

Chapter 16
1. What was the name given to the Bougainville invasion? **Cartwheel.**
2. Why would it be important for the Allies to have a successful invasion of Bougainville? **It would turn the war around because the Allies would be on the offensive rather than the defense.**
3. Give the actual meaning for the following code names:
   A. Alligator: **landing boats**
   B. Men's names: **fighter planes**
   C. Women's names: **bombers**
   D. Zekes: **Zeros- A6M Japanese fighter planes**
   E. Val: **the slow two-engine bombers used by the Japanese**
   F. Kate: **the Japanese torpedo-bomber**
   G. Betty: **the faster Mitsubishi G4M two-engine bomber**
4. Why were nicknames used for planes, bombers, and submarines? **Using common names made it feel less scary for the service men fighting against them.**
5. What obstacle did the Americans face when landing on Empress Augusta Bay on Bougainville? **It was swamp land. It was hard to maneuver through.**
6. Describe the *battle of the Four Sitting Ducks*? **The Marines were defeated by the Japanese at Guadalcanal in 1942 when 4 of their cruisers were destroyed. The Navy retreated which left the Marines on the island with half their supplies and fighting against 50,000 Japanese soldiers.**
7. How did the Marines deal with their nervousness on the morning before the D-day attack? **They tried to have conversations, they sang quietly, they retied their boots, checked their ammunition and equipment. Anything that would take their minds off of what was about to happen.**
8. How does the author build suspense while describing the pre-battle scene of D-day? **Answers will vary.**

Chapter 17
1. How many Marines were in the initial landing? **7,000**
2. Why did Ned carry his radio on his chest? **It would protect him against gun fire.**
3. What prompted the Marines to do what needed to be done once they landed on the beach? **The training they had received took over.**
4. Who had been with Ned when they landed on the beach? **Georgia Boy.**
5. Why hadn't the Japanese been killed in the pre-battle strikes by the planes? **The assault had hit too far away, overhead, or too far inland to do much damage.**
6. At the end of the day, what was the thought that struck Ned concerning the battle? **He hadn't seen a single Japanese soldier.**

Chapter 18
1. Describe the conditions of the area where the Marines were camped? **It was a swampy jungle. The bottoms of the foxholes would fill with water as soon as they were dug. It was very hot and humid on the island.**
2. What is malaria? **It is a disease carried by mosquitoes.**

3. How did Officer Williams ensure the Navajos were taking their Atabrine? **He would put the pill into their mouth and wait until they swallowed. Then he would check their mouth.**

4. What is a banzai attack? **It was when every Japanese soldier would leave their post and attack at once. It was also known as a suicide attack.**

5. Why was night the most dangerous time for the Marines? **It was when the Japanese liked to attack.**

6. What could happen if you left your foxhole during the night? **You would be mistaken for a Japanese soldier and shot.**

7. How had Harry Tsosie been killed? **He had left his foxhole and been shot by another Marine.**

8. How old was Ned on November 10? **He turned 17.**

9. Could you imagine fighting in the Marines at 17? **How would you handle seeing people you knew and didn't know being killed? Answers will vary.**

10. Explain what C-rations were. **They are food packages given to soldiers in the event they were cut off from their platoon.**

11. What did the Japanese start doing with the things they left behind? **They started to booby trap them in an attempt to kill enemy soldiers.**

12. What were four rules of sending messages while in the field? **Send, Receive, Roger, and Move.**

13. Why were the four rules important to follow? **The Japanese were able to locate where the message was sent. They would then send a mortar to that location.**

14. What was the responsibility of the Seabees? **They constructed necessary buildings and structures for the camp.**

15. Which Kennedy did Smitty want to introduce Ned to? **John F. Kennedy.**

Essay Question: Imagine yourself, at seventeen, fighting in a war. Do you think you could handle the horrors you would see, the discipline needed, and the courage to defend your country? Describe the personal traits possessed by you that would help you if you were in the same situation.

Chapter 19

1. What problem was the military facing in regards to the code talkers? **They couldn't find enough Navajos to fill the demand.**

2. Describe the incident that changed the captain's mind about code talkers. **His platoon was being shelled by Americans. When they used the radio to tell the Americans to stop shooting they didn't until Ned sent a message using the Navajos language.**

3. What was a danger for a code talker if he had to deliver a message on foot? **American soldiers might confuse them for a Japanese soldier and kill him.**

4. "Never think that war is a good thing, grandchildren. Though I may be necessary at times to defend our people, war is a sickness that must be cured." Page 139. Explain this quote. **Answers will vary.**

5. What did a lot of Marines, code talkers included, do to forget the horrors they had witnessed on the battlefield? **They drank heavily.**

Chapter 20

1. What did the Marines who had lost their equipment at Saipan do once the fighting grew calm? **They went down to the beach and took the guns and equipment off of the dead soldiers.**

2. What did the Japanese civilians do when they saw the Americans? **They killed themselves and their children.**

3. Why did they act this way? **They believed the propaganda the Japanese government told them about Americans.**

4. How many Americans died between June 15 and July 13 on Saipan? How many Japanese? **3,000 and 20,000.**

5. How does the author release tension in his story? **He uses humorous stories to release the tension.**

Chapter 21

1. What scared Ned on Kwajalein and Eniwetok? **The land crabs.**

2. What did Admiral Conolly do differently at Guam that helped the Marines? **He bombed the Japanese for 13 days, destroying their beach defenses.**

3. Who were the Chamorros? **They were American citizens on Guam.**

4. What happened to the Chamorros if they didn't help the Japanese? **They were shot or put into concentration camps.**

5. "Never forget, grandchildren, that we must always see all other people as human beings, worthy of respect." What does this quote mean and why is it relevant for a book on war? **Answers will vary.**

6. How would you describe the relationship between Smitty and Ned? **It was a relationship built on respect. Smitty also felt he was Ned's protector.**

7. How many Japanese were on Guam? **18,000**

8. When did the Japanese prefer to strike the enemy? **They preferred to strike at night.**

9. How did Ned compare what happened to the Chamorros to what had happened to the Navajos? **He compared their plight to that of the Navajos during The Long Walk, when the Navajos had lost their land to the white man.**

10. Who did the code talkers take care of? **Johnny.**

11. Describe what happened to Charlie Begay. **The other code talkers thought he was dead. They prepared him for burial registration. He wasn't dead. Instead, after going to the hospital, he showed up at the Canal very much alive.**

Essay Question: How do you think Ned deals with the suffering of others given his tribes history of mistreatment by whites? Does it surprise you he did not endure more prejudice while in the Marines? What does this say about the men he fought alongside?

Chapter 22

1. How were the Marines like the vehicles they received to use? **Both were in need of patch work, dropped somewhere, and told to do the best they could with what they had.**

2. How did Ned get injured? **He was shot in the shoulder by a sniper.**

3. Who ran Ned to the medic? **Georgia Boy**

4. What is battle fatigue? **It occurs when the mind can't handle all that has been seen and experienced.**

5. Where did Ned go after he left the hospital? **Back to battle.**

Chapter 23

1. What is DDT? **It is a poison that was used to kill insects.**

2. What other creature was on the island other than the land crabs? **Rats.**

3. What are frogmen? **Divers.**

4. Explain what kamikazes were. **They were Japanese suicide bombers.**

5. Why weren't pictures of dead American soldiers shown to civilians until 1943? **It would have an effect on the morale of civilians.**

6. How did the idea of kamikazes come about? **It came about as a result of ships sent by Kublai Khan being destroyed by a strong wind.**

7. What does Kamikaze mean when translated? **The holy wind.**

8. Why did Japanese men volunteer to be kamikaze pilots? **Answers will vary. The answers should have something to do with loyalty to the empire. The influence of the propaganda put out by the government about how successful the kamikaze missions were against the Americans.**

9. Explain what the Geneva Convention rules were during war. **POW's had to be treated fairly, sheltered, and fed. The Red Cross was supposed to have access to them.**

10. How did the rules from Geneva go against what the Japanese believed? **The Japanese believed it was dishonorable to their country and family to surrender. They should commit suicide or banzai attacks.**

11. Why did the Americans try blockades against Japan? **They hoped Japan would surrender when their food supply ran out.**

12. Where Navajos used in other jobs besides as a code talker? If so, what did they do? **Yes, they were usually put as scouts because they were Indians.**

13. What was usually the nickname for any Indian? **Chief**

Chapter 24

1. Why did the Americans decide they needed Iwo Jima? **They needed an emergency landing strip close to Japan.**

2. Describe Iwo Jima. **It is a small island. It is 4 ½ miles long and 2 ½ miles wide. The Japanese had dug tunnels and built bunkers on the island. Guns were hidden in caves.**

3. How did the Japanese fight differently on Iwo Jima? **They didn't do the banzai attacks. Instead, they stayed hidden in their bunkers.**

4. What was a sennimbari? **It was a piece of cloth that was supposed to protect the wearer from harm.**

Chapter 25

1. Why didn't the bombs dropped on Iwo Jima affect the Japanese soldiers? **The soldiers were buried too deep in the tunnels under rock. They were protected.**

2. What did the Marines find in the tunnels that angered them? **They found canned food that said U.S.A. Food Relief. It was the food donated to Japan by Americans before the war.**

3. How many ships sailed to Iwo Jima? **464.**
4. Why did the cooks tell the Marines to enjoy their last meal before the soldiers were to start an attack? **It was their way of saying good luck.**
5. Why didn't Ned eat before the attack on Iwo Jima? **He wasn't hungry and he didn't want a full belly. It wasn't a good thing to get a bullet in the stomach with a full belly. He also thought he might need the food later.**
6. What response did the Americans receive after they started to bomb Iwo Jima right before the soldiers landed? **They got no response.**
7. How had Iwo Jima been made? **From volcanoes.**
8. Why did Ned think their arrival onto the island had been too easy? **The Japanese didn't try to kill them right away.**

Essay Question: How do you think Ned felt when he saw the canned goods in the Japanese tunnels? Consider the circumstances when he and the other Navajos collected the food for the Japanese.

Chapter 26

1. What happened once the troops had arrived on the beach and climbed the first slope? **The Japanese started to bomb and shoot them.**
2. Describe the smells Ned remembers from Iwo Jima. **He remembers the smell of sulfur from the burning gasoline, napalm bombs, gunpowder, and men.**
3. What was the major objective on the island? **To capture Mount Suribachi.**
4. Why was the raising of the American flag so significant to the Marines who saw it flying? **It gave them hope. They thought they had won the island.**
5. How many Marines were injured at Iwo Jima? **6,821**
6. What does Ned mean when he says, "I say "too many" because having a lot of friends during war can be a painful thing?" **Answers will vary.**
7. What happened to Georgia Boy? **He was shot in the neck.**
8. Why didn't medics where the red cross symbol? **The Japanese didn't follow the rules of war and avoid shooting them. They saw the red cross as a useful symbol to shoot at.**
9. What did you learn about the famous picture taken at Iwo Jima? **It was actually staged. It was the second picture taken of the American flag being raised.**
10. Why didn't Ira like looking at the picture of the flag being raised at Iwo Jima? **It reminded him of the men who had been wounded. He heard their voices from the battle at Iwo Jima.**

Chapter 27

1. Why was Iwo Jima considered the key to the war ending? **It allowed a place for the Americans to refuel and make emergency landings close to Japan.**
2. Where was Ned sent after Iwo Jima? **He was sent to the island of Okinawa.**
3. Who was Ned happy to see on the ship? **Georgia Boy.**
4. Why did the landing on Okinawa beaches make the Marines nervous? **They didn't know if it would be a repeat of Iwo Jima when the Japanese waited until a large amount of Marines were on the beach before they started to shoot.**
5. What was the plan of the Japanese on Okinawa? **They were waiting for the Marines to get to Kakazu Ridge before they started their attack.**

6. How many men did the Japanese lose on Okinawa? **110,000.**
7. What was the Thought Police? **It was a way for the government to get rid of people who said negative things about the government.**
8. What was contained in the package sent to the Emperor by the dead soldier's family? **The dead soldier's right index finger.**
9. What did this act of the parents symbolize? **It was equivalent to pointing their finger at the Emperor.**
10. Who was the real power in Japan during the war? **The Supreme Military Council.**
11. Who was the president during the war? **FDR, Franklin Delano Roosevelt**

Chapter 28

1. What events caused Emperor Hirohito to go to the Supreme Council and agree to surrender? **The atomic bombing of Nagasaki and Hiroshima.**
2. What was the date that Japan surrendered to America? **August 15, 1945**
3. What did the code talkers do after hearing about the surrender? **They started to cheer and dance.**

Chapter 29

1. What had the bombs done to the buildings and people of Japan? **Buildings were completely destroyed. The people were burned severely.**
2. What was the designated code for the code talkers? **642**
3. How was Ned treated, while wearing his uniform, when he entered a bar? **The bartender was very rude to him and refused to serve him.**
4. What did Ned realize after his incident at the bar? **Things had not changed in America for people who were not white.**
5. What had Ned learned in the Marines? **He had learned to be self-confident and to believe in himself.**
6. What did Ned mean when he said he needed to heal after the war? **He had seen so many horrors that his mind needed time to heal and accept what he had experienced.**
7. What occupation did Ned do after the war? **He was a teacher.**
8. Why couldn't the Indians use the G.I. Bill to build a new home? **They lived on the reservation and were refused help.**
9. When were the code talkers allowed to discuss their contribution to the war? **In 1969.**

Essay Question: How do you feel about the fact that the Navajos were good enough to lose their lives fighting for the United States, but they were still discriminated against after the war? Explain your answer.

Quizzes and Comprehension Test

Directions: Choose the best answer for each question.

1.   What did the Navajos agree to so they could return to their home?
   A.   They had to learn the white-man ways.
   B.   They had to stop raiding other people.
   C.   They had to obey the American laws.
   D.   All of the above are correct.

2.   The Navajo jewelry symbolized-
   A.   the wealth the Navajo had accumulated from their raids.
   B.   their desire to own pretty things.
   C.   the love their family had for them.
   D.   the wealth they had earned from their creativeness.

3.   Why did the principal of the school believe the children were being disrespectful to him?
   A.   They were yelling at him while he spoke.
   B.   They were looking at the ground while he talked.
   C.   They were ignoring what he was telling them.
   D.   They refused to follow his directions.

4.   What was significant about the Navajos not being allowed to speak their language?
   A.   They were being forced to follow the white-man's ways.
   B.   They were told their language was worthless.
   C.   The kids were being forced to forget their families because they couldn't speak to them.
   D.   The Navajos were separated from their friends.

5.   Why did the school make the Navajo children wear uniforms and get their hair cut?
   A.   The school was trying to help the Navajo children by providing clothes to them.
   B.   The Navajo children were from poor families who couldn't afford proper clothing.
   C.   The Navajo children would appear to be more American.
   D.   The school didn't like the way the children behaved while dressing in traditional Navajo clothes.

6. Who is the narrator of the story?
   A. Principal O'Sullivan
   B. John Reamer
   C. John Roanhorse
   D. Ned Begay

7. How did the Navajo children disobey the teachers at the school?
   A. They refused to go by their American name.
   B. They stopped going to classes.
   C. They spoke Navajo when teachers weren't around to hear.
   D. They wore their jewelry under their clothes.

8. Why did the narrator resent the way the teachers treated him?
   A. He didn't like that they refused to use his Navajo name when calling upon him.
   B. He believed they thought he was not as smart as white children.
   C. He resented that they didn't respect his beliefs.
   D. He was angry with the way they treated his parents.

9. What is the major theme of the story?
   A. Love
   B. Good vs. Bad
   C. Survival
   D. Friendship

10. What is significant about the Navajos collecting food for the poor people of Japan?
    A. The Japanese had supplied food for the Navajos during their forced walk.
    B. The Navajos did not like the Japanese.
    C. The Navajos were as poor as the Japanese.
    D. The Japanese had always treated the Navajos with disrespect.

11. Who was an ally of Japan?
    A. France
    B. Russia
    C. China
    D. Germany

12. Who was Jim Thorpe?
    A. He was a famous Indian athlete.
    B. He was the principal of the school.
    C. He was the narrator's best friend.
    D. He was a teacher at the high school.

13. What did the narrator believe was his only way to succeed and help his people?
    A. He believed he needed to join the army and prove the worth of the Navajo people.
    B. He believed earning an education was the road to success.
    C. He believed it was his duty to fight the white-man ways in order to reclaim his Navajo culture.
    D. He believed it was crucial that he retain his Navajo language to beat the Americans.

14. What happened to the Navajo children who continued to speak their native language?
    A. They were beaten with a stick.
    B. They were sent home.
    C. They were given additional chores to complete.
    D. They were forced to speak English with an instructor for hours.

15. Who made up the Axis powers?
    A. Japan, China, and Italy
    B. Japan, Germany, and Italy
    C. Germany, Japan, and Russia
    D. Germany, Japan, and China

16. What prevented most Navajos from fighting against Japan?
    A. They weren't fluent in English.
    B. The Navajos were a peaceful nation and didn't believe in fighting.
    C. The Navajos were afraid of the Japanese because they looked similar to Indians.
    D. They had not gone through the training to be Americans.

17. What problem did the Navajos run into when they tried to sign up for the Marines?
    A. They were too short.
    B. They didn't have a birth certificate to prove their age.
    C. Their parents wouldn't let them join because of the history of poor treatment toward the Navajos.
    D. The Navajo men didn't know how to shoot a gun.

18. Why did the narrator believe in First Sergeant Shinn?
    A. Shinn told him what he wanted to hear.
    B. Shinn promised that all the Navajos could fight for America.
    C. The narrator and Shinn had come from the same reservation.
    D. The narrator had observed how Shinn carried himself and spoke about the Marines.

19. Why wasn't the narrator allowed to join the Marines when First Sergeant Shinn was there?
    A. Shinn knew he was too young to join the marines.
    B. The narrator had told Shinn he wasn't old enough to join.
    C. The narrator's parents told him to wait a year.
    D. Shinn had spoken to the narrator's parents about the Marines.

20. The narrator's desire to join the Marines conveys-
    A. his dislike for the Germans.
    B. his pride in America.
    C. his anger toward the treatment of Indians everywhere.
    D. his enjoyment of being a Navajo Indian.

Code Talker Quiz 2
Chapters 8 – 15

Directions: Choose the best answer for each question.

1.   Why were the families of the Navajo Marines worried about their sons?
    A.   They were afraid the Marines would harm them.
    B.   They had not heard from their sons since they had left.
    C.   The letters they had written to their sons had been returned.
    D.   They were not allowed to visit their sons in boot camp.

2.   Ned was not surprised none of the Navajos washed out of boot camp because
    A.   he believed Navajos were superior to the other Marines.
    B.   he and the Navajos were used to cheating to get what they wanted.
    C.   the Navajos were used to the work associated with the boot camp.
    D.   boot camp was much harder than he had expected.

3.   What ceremony was performed on Ned that would provide safety to him?
    A.   Communion ceremony
    B.   Baptismal ceremony
    C.   Blessingway ceremony
    D.   Dinas' ceremony

4.   Ned's feelings the next day after the ceremony conveys
    A.   the importance of peace and balance within a Navajo.
    B.   the belief of ceremonies to survive the day.
    C.   the need for ceremonies whenever possible.
    D.   the significance of pollen and its potency.

5.   What was important about Fort Defiance?
    A.   It was where Ned's parents had met each other.
    B.   It was the place where Navajos had ended up after the Long Walk.
    C.   It was the fort that most Navajos had traded at long ago.
    D.   It was the starting point of the Long Walk.

Code Talker Quiz 2
Chapters 8 – 15

6. How did the first day of boot camp compare to the first day of school?
   A. The Navajos were treated unfairly.
   B. The Navajos had their heads shaved and where given a uniform to wear.
   C. The other Marines treated them poorly.
   D. The other Marines laughed at them.

7. Why did Ned dislike boxing?
   A. It felt unnatural for him to hit another human being.
   B. He wasn't very good at it.
   C. Ned was very good at boxing which troubled his peaceful mind.
   D. Ned was constantly being beat by the other Marines.

8. How does the author change the mood of the story by telling about Ned's experience of learning to swim?
   A. The author uses fear of failing to convey the sense of urgency in Ned.
   B. The author uses humor to release the tension built up through the telling of the "sink or swim" ordeal.
   C. The author uses sarcasm to create a mood of camaraderie among the Navajos.
   D. The author uses figurative language to create a mental picture of the cruelty of the Marines.

9. What did Ned learn about white men during boot camp?
   A. White men were mean to Navajos.
   B. White men were more intelligent than Navajos.
   C. White men were no different than anyone else.
   D. White men knew everything.

10. Where did the term *leathernecks* come from?
   A. The Army provided their soldiers with neck protectors made out of leather.
   B. The Marines were the toughest of all the armed forces.
   C. The Marines were known for their stubbornness toward Navajos.
   D. The Marines were the men who held the Army soldiers together.

Code Talker Quiz 2
Chapters 8 – 15

11. Why were the Navajo Marines put into a barrack with barred windows and a locked door?
    A. The Marines did not trust them.
    B. They were put into the locked barrack for their own protection.
    C. The Navajos were going to learn a top secret program.
    D. The Navajos needed to be protected from those Marines who didn't like Navajos.

12. Why did a new code need to be created?
    A. The Japanese had broken all the other codes used by the United States.
    B. The government realized they needed a new code when they went against Germany.
    C. The new code could be used by every branch of the military.
    D. The government realized the Germans had broken all of their other codes.

13. What can you infer from, "The lives of many men will depend on your messages?"
    A. Winning or losing the War would be the sole responsibility of the code talkers.
    B. The defeat of the Germans would depend on the messages sent and received by the code talkers.
    C. If the Navajos did not send or receive the correct messages every time lives would be lost.
    D. The messages sent by the Navajos needed to be accurate most of the time.

14. Where were the codes used by the Navajos kept?
    A. The codes were kept in a safe at boot camp.
    B. The codes were memorized by the Navajo code talker.
    C. Most of the codes were stored in Washington.
    D. All of the codes were kept in a safe place in Washington.

15. What was a result of the code talker program?
    A. Navajos were never given promotions in the Marines.
    B. Many lives were lost as a result of the program.
    C. The families of the Navajo code talkers were given a better life on the reservation.
    D. The code talkers were treated with the utmost respect when they returned to America.

16. What was the major difference between the Navajo code and the white code?
    A. The white code was more efficient.
    B. The Navajo code was sent quicker than the white code.
    C. The white code was received quicker than the Navajo code.
    D. The Navajo code was sent and received quicker than the white code.

17. What was one belief held by top military personnel in connection with the new code?
    A. The new code would not succeed.
    B. The Navajos would not be able to defend the Germans.
    C. The code would be efficient in the battlefield.
    D. The Navajos would forget the code under the strain of battle.

18. Why were the corpses of the Japanese soldiers unsettling to the Navajos?
    A. The Japanese soldiers looked a lot like the Navajos.
    B. The dead bodies brought diseases.
    C. The Navajos believed bad spirits surrounded a dead body.
    D. The Navajos believed a body should be buried to rid itself of this world.

19. Which example demonstrates the knowledge the Navajos contained about survival?
    A. The Navajos knew to run only at night when it wasn't too hot.
    B. The Navajos had experienced fights with enemies for centuries.
    C. The Navajos knew to drink the cactus juice to survive in the desert.
    D. The Navajos knew that snakes led the way to water.

20. Why did Ned disagree with the practice runs on Guadalcanal?
    A. Ned didn't think the code talkers were given enough time to send messages.
    B. The island was covered with crocodiles, leeches, spiders, and poisonous centipedes.
    C. The soldiers were not equipped with guns and ammunition on the practice runs.
    D. The practice runs were not filled with chaos like a real battle.

Code Talker Quiz 3
Chapters 16 – 22

Directions: Choose the best answer for each question.

1. The Allies needed to be successful on Bougainville because
   A. the people back home thought they were losing the war against Germany.
   B. the Allies would be on the offensive rather than defensive.
   C. The Japanese were losing hope they would win the war.
   D. Germany was becoming too powerful.

2. What effect did giving nicknames to bombers and planes have on the soldiers?
   A. The soldiers were better able to shoot them down.
   B. The names made the bombers and planes seem less scary.
   C. The soldiers were able to laugh about them.
   D. The names made the bombers and planes easier to identify.

3. How does the author build suspense for the pre-battle scene of D-day?
   A. The author uses humor to add suspense.
   B. The author conveys the sense of unease by describing the nervousness of the soldiers.
   C. The author illustrates suspense by retelling the death toll that will take place.
   D. The author demonstrates the feeling of suspense by detailing the job of the code talkers.

4. How had the training the Marines helped them during the landing of D-day?
   A. The soldiers knew what had to be done instinctively because they had practiced the maneuvers so often.
   B. The soldiers continued to look to their commanders for directions once they had landed.
   C. The soldiers hesitated on D-day because they were unsure what they should do after landing.
   D. The soldiers relied on the code talkers to give them directions, just like during training.

5. What is malaria?
   A. It was a technique used by the Japanese to avoid detection.
   B. It was a strategic maneuver used during the invasion of D-day.
   C. It was a disease carried by mosquitoes.
   D. It was the inflammation or swelling of their fingers due to the humid conditions of the jungle.

6. How did the conditions of the jungle impact the soldiers?
   A. The fox holes needed for protection would fill with water making the soldiers uncomfortable.
   B. The soldiers were unable to see due to the blowing of the sand into their eyes.
   C. The hot sun caused a lot of soldiers to become sick.
   D. The humidity prevented the soldiers from identifying the Japanese soldiers.

7. Why did Officer Williams force the Navajos to take Atabrine?
   A. Atabrine was used to ward off mosquitoes.
   B. The Navajos refused to take the Atabrine because it gave them headaches.
   C. Officer Williams had to force the Navajos to take Atabrine because it was an experimental drug.
   D. It was necessary for the Navajos to take Atabrine so they wouldn't get a disease.

8. What risk would a soldier be taking if they left their foxhole at night?
   A. The soldier would get lost.
   B. The soldier would fall into someone else's foxhole.
   C. The soldier might get hurt wandering around at night.
   D. The soldier might be mistaken for an enemy and be shot.

9. Food portions given to soldiers in the event they were separated from their platoon were
   A. Ready Pacs
   B. Real Meals
   C. C-rations
   D. Kamikazis

10. What did soldiers need to be aware of if they found items left by the Japanese?
    A. The soldiers needed to make sure they had the room to store the item.
    B. The soldiers needed to watch for booby traps.
    C. The soldiers should be aware of any and all items that would be useful to them.
    D. The soldiers needed to remember that guns and ammunition were key finds and should be taken.

11. Why was the last directive of "send, receive, roger, and move" so important for the code talker to follow?
    A. The code talker needed to keep on the move so more messages could be sent.
    B. The Japanese would try to prevent the code talker from sending additional messages by cornering him in one location.
    C. The code talker was also responsible for hand delivering messages as quickly as possible.
    D. The Japanese would send a mortar shell to the last place a message was sent/received from.

12. What problem arose due to the success of the Navajo code talkers?
    A. The Navajo code talkers demanded higher pay.
    B. The government could not find enough Navajos to fill demand.
    C. The government refused to accept the Navajos as real Marines.
    D. The Navajos demanded they be promoted once they realized their worth to the government.

13. What danger existed for a code talker who had to deliver a message by foot?
    A. He might be shot after being confused for a Japanese soldier.
    B. He might get hurt from running across rough terrain.
    C. The code talker might get lost in the confusion of battle.
    D. The code talker runs the risk of falling into a foxhole.

14. Why did the Japanese civilians kill themselves when they lost Saipan?
    A. They thought the end of the world had occurred.
    B. The Japanese people felt ashamed at their loss.
    C. They did not want the Americans to torture them into telling government secrets.
    D. The Japanese people believed the propaganda they had been told concerning the American soldiers.

15. What happened to the Chamorros if they refused to help the Japanese?
    A. The Chamorros were Japanese natives on Guam who were treated very well.
    B. The Chamorros were sent to concentration camps if they refused to help the Japanese.
    C. The Chamorros were native people of Guam who were not used during the battle on Guam.
    D. The Chamorros were Japanese citizens who were shot for refusing to help their brothers.

16. What was the relationship between Smitty and Ned?
    A. They were enemies because Smitty had made fun of Ned during boot camp.
    B. Smitty was Ned's cousin from the reservation.
    C. Smitty believed he was Ned's protector.
    D. Ned was Smitty's protector.

17. What tactic did the Japanese like to use while on the island of Guam?
    A. They liked to attack at night.
    B. They liked to booby trap the foxholes dug by the Americans.
    C. The Japanese used grenades tied to tree branches near the foxholes.
    D. The Japanese soldiers would dress like American soldiers and sneak into the American's camp.

18. What did the Marine's equipment and the Marines themselves have in common?
    A. Both were tough.
    B. Both were the best of the best.
    C. Both needed patch work and were expected to perform the best they could.
    D. Both had been abused by the government.

19. Who was responsible for running Ned to the medic after he had been wounded?
    A. Smitty
    B. Georgia Boy
    C. Ned took himself to the medic.
    D. Harry

20. What comparison could be made between the Navajos and the Chamorros?
    A. Both groups had lost land and home to the white man.
    B. Both groups were used by the white man to benefit the white man.
    C. Both groups were related to the Japanese.
    D. Both groups were fighting in a war they did not believe in.

Code Talker Comprehension Test
Chapters 1- 29

1. What did the Navajos agree to so they could return to their home?
   A. They had to learn the white-man ways.
   B. They had to stop raiding other people.
   C. They had to obey the American laws.
   D. All of the above are correct.

2. The Navajo jewelry symbolized-
   A. the wealth the Navajo had accumulated from their raids.
   B. their desire to own pretty things.
   C. the love their family had for them.
   D. the wealth they had earned from their creativeness.

3. Why did the principal of the school believe the children were being disrespectful to him?
   A. They were yelling at him while he spoke.
   B. They were looking at the ground while he talked.
   C. They were ignoring what he was telling them.
   D. They refused to follow his directions.

4. What was significant about the Navajos not being allowed to speak their language?
   A. They were being forced to follow the white-man's ways.
   B. They were told their language was worthless.
   C. The kids were forced to forget their families because they couldn't speak to them.
   D. The Navajos were separated from their friends.

5. Why did the school make the Navajo children wear uniforms and get their hair cut?
   A. The school was trying to help the Navajo children by providing clothes to them.
   B. The Navajo children were from poor families who couldn't afford proper clothing.
   C. The Navajo children would appear to be more American.
   D. The school didn't like the way the children behaved while dressing in traditional Navajo clothes.

6. What did Ned believe was his only way to succeed and help his people?
   A. He believed he needed to join the army and prove the worth of the Navajo people.
   B. He believed earning an education was the road to success.
   C. He believed it was his duty to fight the white-man ways in order to reclaim his Navajo culture.
   D. He believed it was crucial that he retain his Navajo language to beat the Americans.

7. What happened to the Navajo children who continued to speak their native language?
   A. They were beaten with a stick.
   B. They were sent home.
   C. They were given additional chores to complete.
   D. They were forced to speak English with an instructor for hours.

8. Who made up the Axis powers?
   A. Japan, China, and Italy
   B. Germany, Japan, and China
   C. Germany, Japan, and Russia
   D. Japan, Germany, and Italy

9. What prevented most Navajos from fighting against Japan?
   A. They weren't fluent in English.
   B. The Navajos were a peaceful nation and didn't believe in fighting.
   C. The Navajos were afraid of the Japanese because they looked similar to Indians.
   D. They had not gone through the training to be Americans.

10. What problem did the Navajos run into when they tried to sign up for the Marines?
    A. They were too short.
    B. They didn't have a birth certificate to prove their age.
    C. Their parents wouldn't let them join because of the history of poor treatment toward the Navajos.
    D. The Navajo men didn't know how to shoot a gun.

11. Why did Ned believe in First Sergeant Shinn when he first came to recruit the Navajos?
    A.   Shinn told him what he wanted to hear.
    B.   Shinn promised that all the Navajos could fight for America.
    C.   The narrator had observed how Shinn carried himself and spoke about the Marines.
    D.   The narrator and Shinn had come from the same reservation.

12. Why wasn't Ned allowed to join the Marines when First Sergeant Shinn was there?
    A.   Shinn knew he was too young to join the marines.
    B.   Ned had told Shinn he wasn't old enough to join.
    C.   Ned parents told him to wait a year.
    D.   Shinn had spoken to the narrator's parents about the Marines.

13. Ned's desire to join the Marines conveys-
    A.   his dislike for the Germans.
    B.   his pride in America.
    C.   his anger toward the treatment of Indians everywhere.
    D.   his enjoyment of being a Navajo Indian.

14. How does the author change the mood of the story by telling about Ned's experience of learning to swim?
    A.   The author uses humor to release the tension built up through the telling of the "sink or swim" ordeal.
    B.   The author uses fear of failing to convey the sense of urgency in Ned.
    C.   The author uses sarcasm to create a mood of camaraderie among the Navajos.
    D.   The author uses figurative language to create a mental picture of the cruelty of the Marines.

15. What did Ned learn about white men during boot camp?
    A.   White men were mean to Navajos.
    B.   White men were more intelligent than Navajos.
    C.   White men knew everything.
    D.   White men were no different than anyone else.

16. What was the major difference between the Navajo code and the white code?
    A.   The white code was more efficient.
    B.   The Navajo code was sent quicker than the white code.
    C.   The white code was received quicker than the Navajo code.
    D.   The Navajo code was sent and received quicker than the white code.

17. What was one belief held by top military personnel in connection with the new code?
    A.   The new code would not succeed.
    B.   The Navajos would not be able to defend the Germans.
    C.   The code would be efficient in the battlefield.
    D.   The Navajos would forget the code under the strain of battle.

18. Why were the corpses of the Japanese soldiers unsettling to the Navajos?
    A.   The Japanese soldiers looked a lot like the Navajos.
    B.   The dead bodies brought diseases.
    C.   The Navajos believed bad spirits surrounded a dead body.
    D.   The Navajos believed a body should be buried to rid itself of this world.

19. Which example demonstrates the knowledge the Navajos contained about survival?
    A.   The Navajos knew to run only at night when it wasn't too hot.
    B.   The Navajos had experienced fights with enemies for centuries.
    C.   The Navajos knew to drink the cactus juice to survive in the desert.
    D.   The Navajos knew that snakes led the way to water.

20. Why did Ned disagree with the practice runs on Guadalcanal?
    A.   Ned didn't think the code talkers were given enough time to send messages.
    B.   The island was covered with crocodiles, leeches, spiders, and poisonous centipedes.
    C.   The soldiers were not equipped with guns and ammunition on the practice runs.
    D.   The practice runs were not filled with chaos like a real battle.

21. What effect did giving nicknames to bombers and planes have on the soldiers?
    A. The soldiers were better able to shoot them down.
    B. The names made the bombers and planes seem less scary.
    C. The soldiers were able to laugh about them.
    D. The names made the bombers and planes easier to identify.

22. How does the author build suspense for the pre-battle scene of D-day?
    A. The author conveys the sense of unease by describing the nervousness of the soldiers.
    B. The author uses humor to add suspense.
    C. The author illustrates suspense by retelling the death toll that will take place.
    D. The author demonstrates the feeling of suspense by detailing the job of the code talkers.

23. How had the training the Marines helped them during the landing of D-day?
    A. The soldiers knew what had to be done instinctively because they had practiced the maneuvers so often.
    B. The soldiers continued to look to their commanders for directions once they had landed.
    C. The soldiers hesitated on D-day because they were unsure what they should do after landing.
    D. The soldiers relied on the code talkers to give them directions, just like during training.

24. What is malaria?
    A. It was a technique used by the Japanese to avoid detection.
    B. It was a strategic maneuver used during the invasion of D-day.
    C. It was a disease carried by mosquitoes.
    D. It was the inflammation or swelling of their fingers due to the humid conditions of the jungle.

25. Why was the last directive of "send, receive, roger, and move" so important for the code talker to follow?
    A. The code talker needed to keep on the move so more messages could be sent.
    B. The Japanese would try to prevent the code talker from sending additional messages by cornering him in one location.
    C. The code talker was also responsible for hand delivering messages as quickly as possible.
    D. The Japanese would send a mortar shell to the last place a message was sent/received from.

26. What problem arose due to the success of the Navajo code talkers?
    A. The Navajo code talkers demanded higher pay.
    B. The government could not find enough Navajos to fill demand.
    C. The government refused to accept the Navajos as real Marines.
    D. The Navajos demanded they be promoted once they realized their worth to the government.

27. What danger existed for a code talker who had to deliver a message by foot?
    A. He might be shot after being confused for a Japanese soldier.
    B. He might get hurt from running across rough terrain.
    C. The code talker might get lost in the confusion of battle.
    D. The code talker runs the risk of falling into a foxhole.

28. Why did the Japanese civilians kill themselves when they lost Saipan?
    A. They thought the end of the world had occurred.
    B. The Japanese people felt ashamed at their loss.
    C. They did not want the Americans to torture them into telling government secrets.
    D. The Japanese people believed the propaganda they had been told concerning the American soldiers.

29. What effect would showing pictures of dead American soldiers have on the American public?
    A. The American public would have been demoralized by the pictures.
    B. The American public would have become angrier at Japan.
    C. The American public would have sought revenge against Japan after the war was over.
    D. The American public would have given up the fight against Japan.

30. Why did American's fear kamikazes?
    A. Kamikazes were Japanese spies in America.
    B. Kamikazes could not be stopped because they were on a suicide mission.
    C. Americans feared kamikazes because they spread disease.
    D. American soldiers did not fear kamikazes because the soldiers knew they could be defeated.

31. Why were the Geneva Convention rules so important?
    A. In war, rules had to be followed or chaos would reign.
    B. The rules state how soldiers should be treated during battle.
    C. The rules of the Geneva Convention were put in place to protect Prisoners of War.
    D. The rules safe guarded civilians during war.

32. Why did the Japanese **not** believe in the rules of the Geneva Convention?
    A. The Japanese believed all was fair in war time.
    B. The Japanese thought the rules were unfair to the Japanese.
    C. The Japanese believed it was a dishonor to surrender to the enemy.
    D. The Japanese thought the rules were not meant for their civilians.

33. The reason why Americans needed Iwo Jima was-
    A. They needed an emergency landing strip close to Japan.
    B. They wanted a base in the Pacific to build their atomic bomb.
    C. The Americans wanted to defeat Japan at every possible area.
    D. The Americans needed Iwo Jima to show how strong they had become.

34. What did the Japanese do differently on Iwo Jima that made it difficult to defeat them?
    A. They used banzai attacks against the Americans.
    B. The Japanese attacked the Americans at night.
    C. They attacked the Americans all day long to tire the Americans.
    D. The Japanese dug tunnels and bunkers where they stay hidden.

35. What did the Americans find in the Japanese tunnels that angered them?
    A. They found American made weapons.
    B. The Americans found a code talker manual.
    C. The Americans found a stash of ammunition that had been stolen from them.
    D. They found food given to the Japanese by the Americans before the war began.

36. What did the American flag on Mount Suribachi symbolize to most of the Marines?
    A. It symbolized hope of winning the island.
    B. It symbolized the blood, sweat, and tears that had been lost on the island.
    C. It symbolized the destruction of the Japanese on the island.
    D. It symbolized the end of the war.

37. Who had the real power in Japan during the war?
    A. The Emperor
    B. The kamikaze soldiers
    C. The Supreme Military Council
    D. Parliament

38. What was the result of the bombing of Nagasaki and Hiroshima?
    A. Millions of people died immediately.
    B. Japan surrendered to America.
    C. The Emperor fled Japan.
    D. FDR surrendered to Japan.

39. Upon Ned's return from the war, what did he realize about America?
    A. Many people were still fighting the war against Japan.
    B. The American people were still prejudiced against non-white people.
    C. Americans were very grateful for the service of the Navajos.
    D. The American people respected the Marines more than any other military branch.

40. How many years went by before the code talkers were allowed to discuss their contribution to World War II?
    A. More than 50 years
    B. Less than 20 years
    C. 2 years
    D. Almost 25 years

Answers to Assessments

Quiz 1	Quiz 2	Quiz 3	
1. D	1. B	1. B	10. B
2. C	2. C	2. B	11. C
3. B	3. C	3. B	12. C
4. A	4. A	4. A	13. B
5. C	5. D	5. C	14. A
6. D	6. B	6. A	15. D
7. C	7. A	7. D	16. D
8. B	8. B	8. D	17. A
9. C	9. C	9. C	18. B
10. C	10. B	10. B	19. C
11. D	11. C	11. D	20. D
12. A	12. A	12. B	21. B
13. B	13. C	13. A	22. A
14. A	14. B	14. D	23. A
15. B	15. A	15. B	24. C
16. A	16. D	16. C	25. D
17. B	17. A	17. A	26. B
18. D	18. C	18. C	27. A
19. C	19. C	19. B	28. D
20. B	20. D	20. A	29. A
			30. B
			31. C
		Comprehension	32. C
		Test	33. A
		1. A	34. D
		2. C	35. D
		3. B	36. A
		4. A	37. C
		5. C	38. B
		6. B	39. B
		7. A	40. D
		8. D	
		9. A	

Made in the USA
Columbia, SC
02 July 2018